P9-DFK-320

ELTON JOHN & TIM RICE'S

AIDA

In Australia Contact:

Hal Leonard Australia Pty. Ltd.
22 Taunton Drive P.O. Box 5130
Cheltenham East, 3192 Victoria, Australia
Email: ausadmin@halleonard.com

ISBN 0-634-05420-1

Wonderland Music Company, Inc.

DISTRIBUTED BY

HAL•LEONARD®
CORPORATION

7777 W. BLUEMOUND RD. P.O. BOX 13819 MILWAUKEE, WI 53213

Visit Hal Leonard Online at
www.halleonard.com

EVERY STORY IS A LOVE STORY

Music by ELTON JOHN
Lyrics by TIM RICE

In 2

Gentle 2 (♩ = 82)

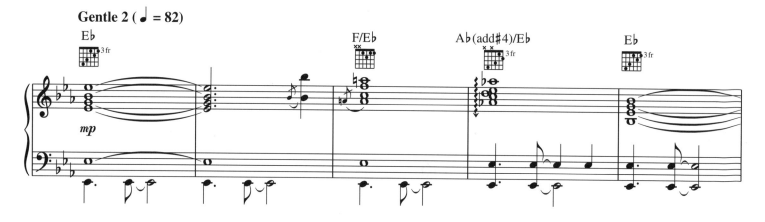

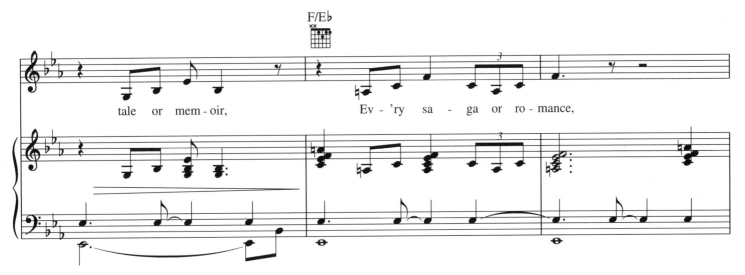

tale or mem-oir, Ev-'ry sa-ga or ro-mance,

Wheth-er true or fab-ri-cat-ed, Wheth-er planned ___ or

hap-pen-stance ___

Wheth-er sweep-ing through the ag-es, cast-ing cen-tu-ries a-

THE PAST IS ANOTHER LAND

Music by ELTON JOHN
Lyrics by TIM RICE

sess   The past   is now an-oth-er land

far be-yond my __ reach __   In-vad-ed by in-sid-ious for-eign

bod-ies   for-eign speech   Where the time-less joys of child-hood   Lie

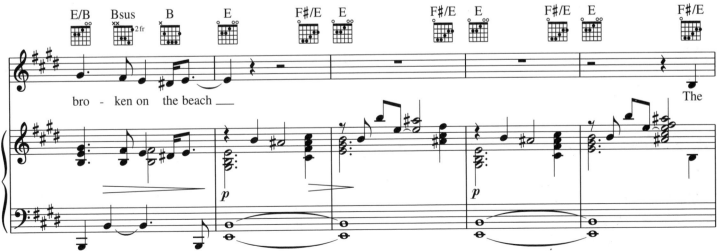

bro-ken on the beach __   The

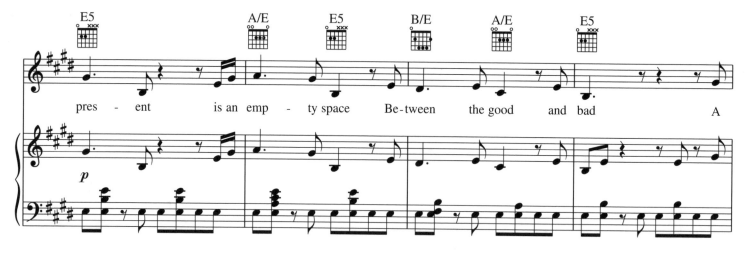

pres - ent is an emp - ty space Be - tween the good and bad A

mo - ment lead - ing no - where Too point - less to be sad __ But

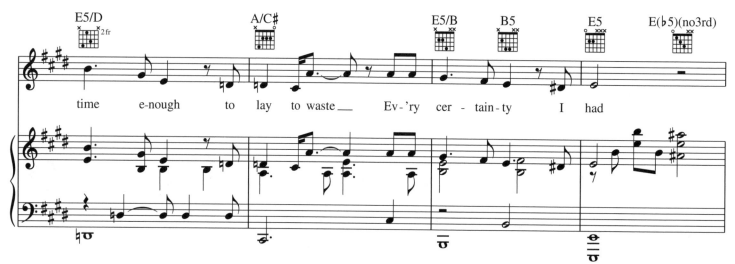

time e - nough to lay to waste __ Ev - 'ry cer - tain - ty I had

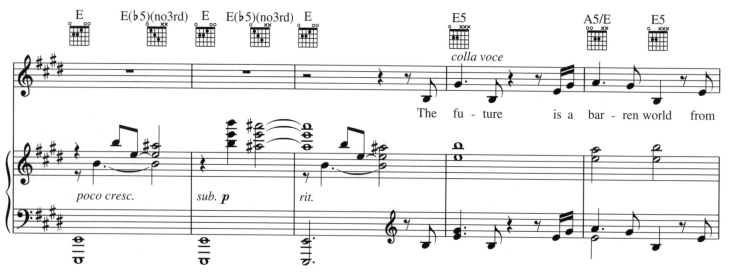

The fu - ture is a bar - ren world from

HOW I KNOW YOU

Music by ELTON JOHN
Lyrics by TIM RICE

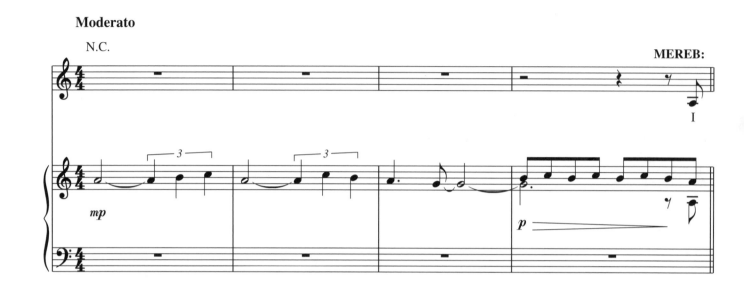

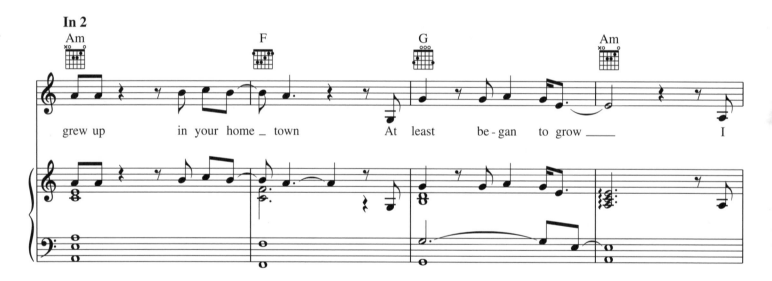

you That spark of hope — for free - dom No

ter - ror can sub - due ___ My on - ly hope is si -

AIDA:

- lence ___ You've ___ nev - er seen my face No

you re - main a prin - cess In an - y time ___ or place ___

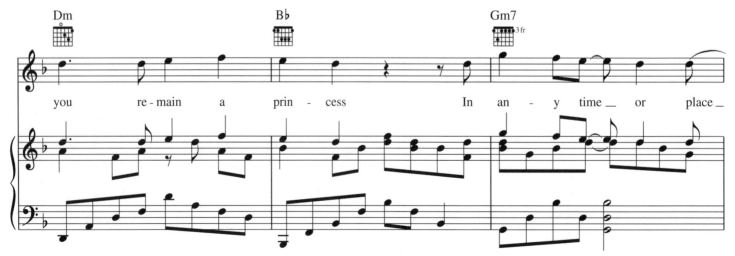

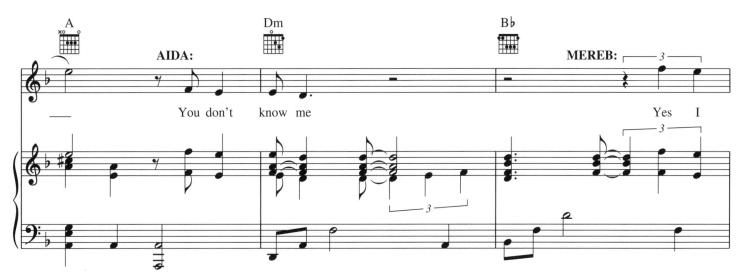

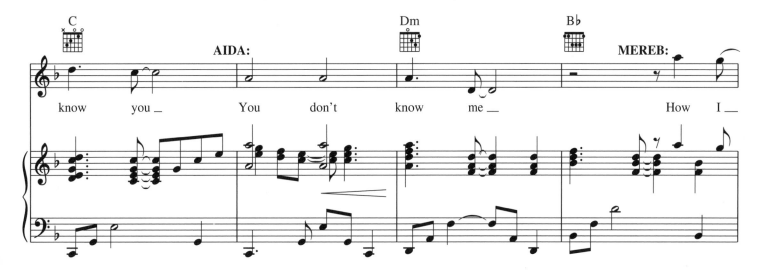

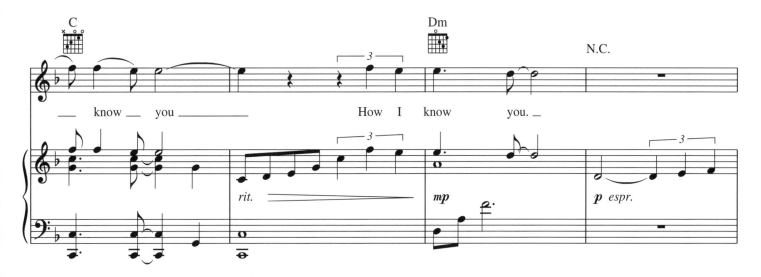

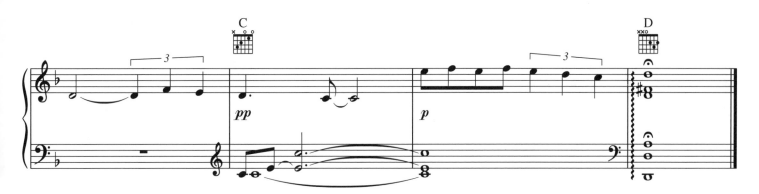

NOT ME

Music by ELTON JOHN
Lyrics by TIM RICE

will say ____ "Not ____ me"? ____

This can nev - er

Not __ me ____

be ____

He's in love ____ but he's

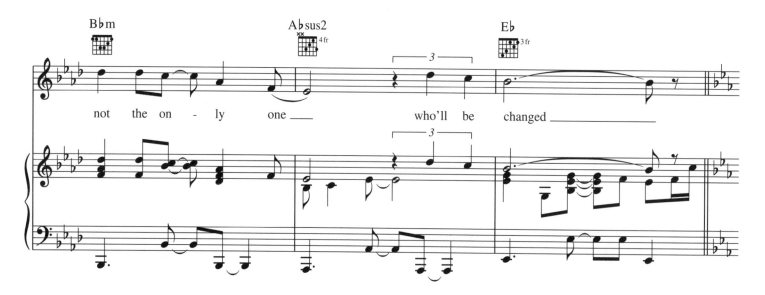

not the on - ly one ____ who'll be changed ____

AMNERIS:
(Spoken:) Why hasn't Radames come to see me again? We're to be married in three days, and yet, Aida, I must make

things right with him.

Repeat if needed   AIDA:
I shall not en - vy lov - ers ___ But

AMNERIS:
long ___ for what they share ___ An emp-ty room is mer - ci - less ___

Don't be sur - prised ___ if I con - fess ___ I need some com - fort there ___

AIDA & AMNERIS:

And who'd have thought _ our love _

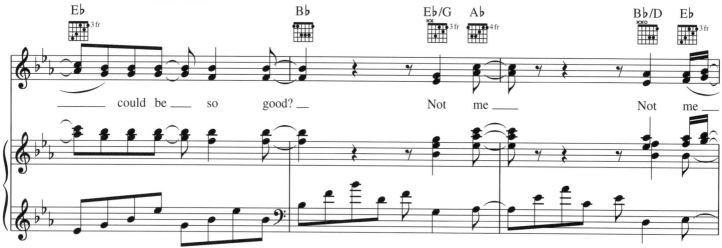

_____ could be _ so good? _ Not me _____ Not me _____

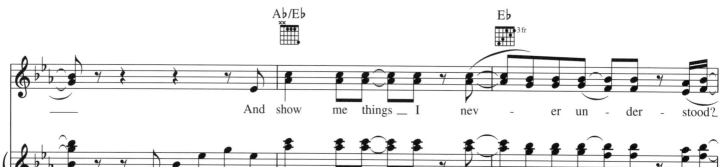

And show me things _ I nev - er un - der - stood?

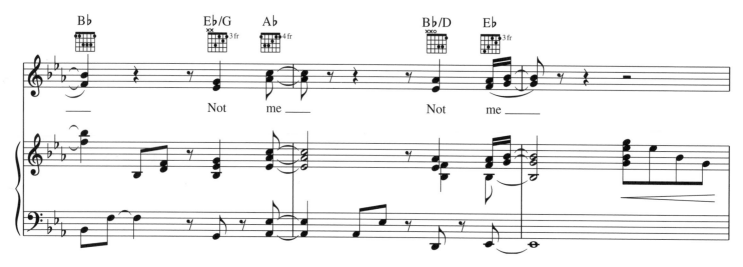

Not me _____ Not me _____

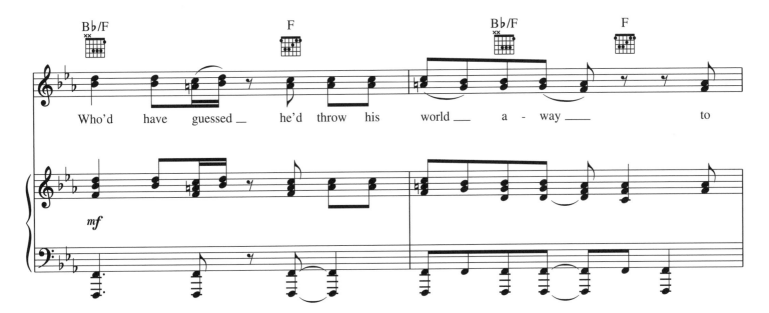

Who'd have guessed __ he'd throw his world __ a - way __ to

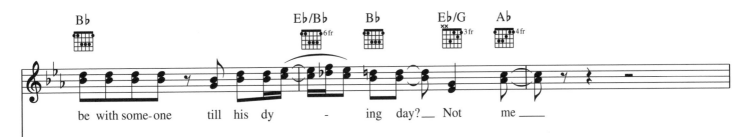

be with some-one till his dy - ing day?__ Not me __

Not me __

RADAMES:

And

And

ELABORATE LIVES

Music by ELTON JOHN
Lyrics by TIM RICE

A STEP TOO FAR

Music by ELTON JOHN
Lyrics by TIM RICE

Moderately fast

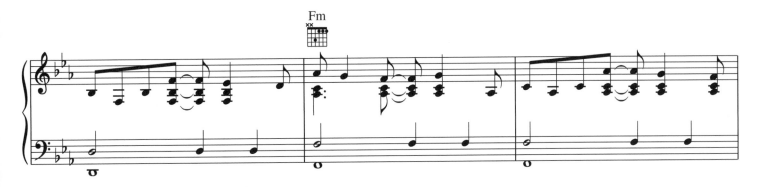

AMNERIS:

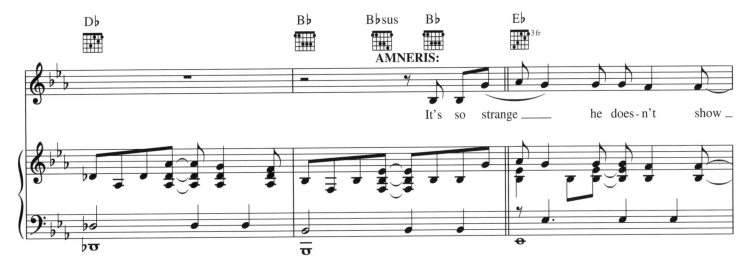

It's so strange _____ he does-n't show _____

_____ me _____ More af - fec - tion than he needs   Al - most

half __ a step be - hind ___ O _____ ho _____

O _____ ho _____

O _____ ho _____

RADAMES:

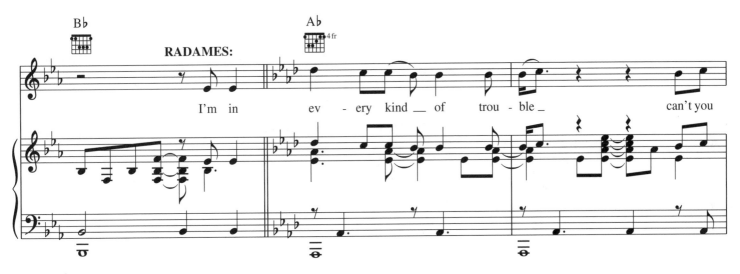

I'm in ev - ery kind __ of trou - ble __ can't you

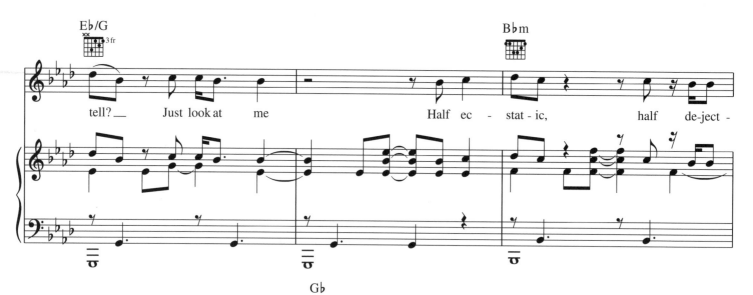

turned on its head   Of a life _____ turned on its head _____

O _____ ho _____

RADAMES:

AMNERIS: O _____ ho _____   O _____ ho _____

AIDA:

O _____ ho _____   I am

lead - er? Am I trai - tor? _____ Did I take a step too far? _

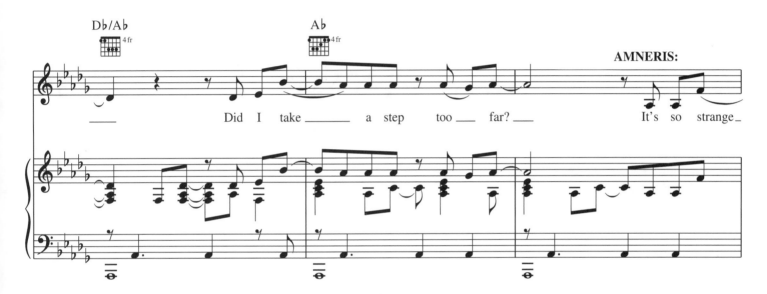

_____ Did I take _____ a step too _____ far? _____

AMNERIS:
It's so strange _

_____ he does-n't show ___ me _ More af - fec - tion than he needs

AIDA:
I am cer - tain that ___ I love _

RADAMES:
I'm in ev - ery kind _ of trou - ble _ can't you

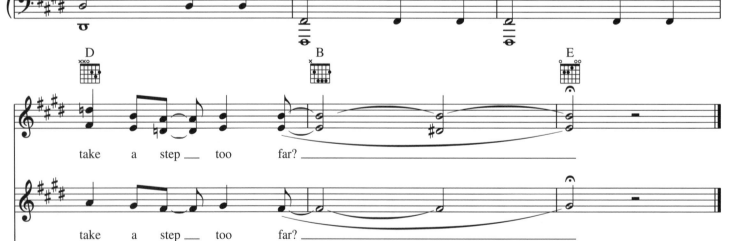

EASY AS LIFE

Music by ELTON JOHN
Lyrics by TIM RICE

Pas - sion would have cooled and all the mag - ic would have died.

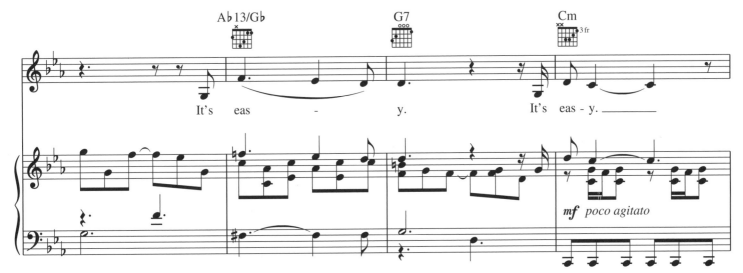

It's eas - y. It's eas-y. _____

mf poco agitato

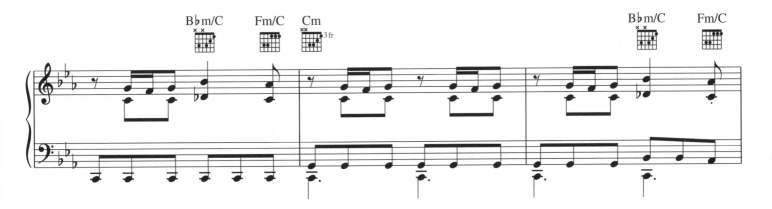

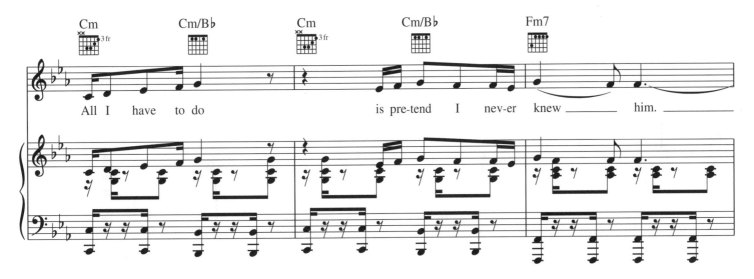

All I have to do is pre-tend I nev-er knew _____ him. _____

LIKE FATHER, LIKE SON

Music by ELTON JOHN
Lyrics by TIM RICE

At times ac-claimed, at times ____ re-viled you'll wind up do-ing just what I'd have done._

PRIESTS: son._

Like Fa-ther like __ son._

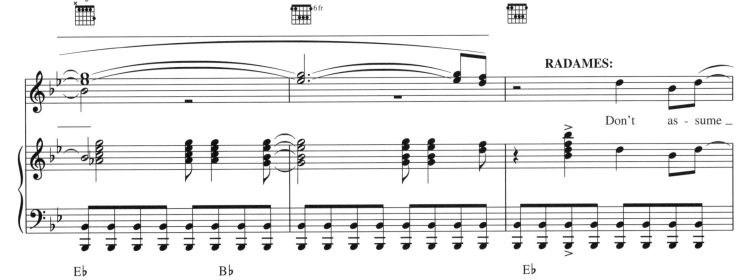

RADAMES:

Don't as-sume _

_____ your vic-es get __ hand-ed down _____ the line. _

62

the squal-or   at which you ____ ex - cel. ___   It is - n't ver - y hard ___

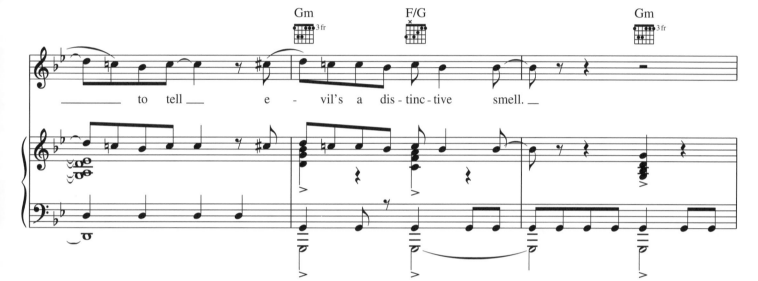

____ to tell ___ e - vil's a - dis - tinc - tive smell. ___

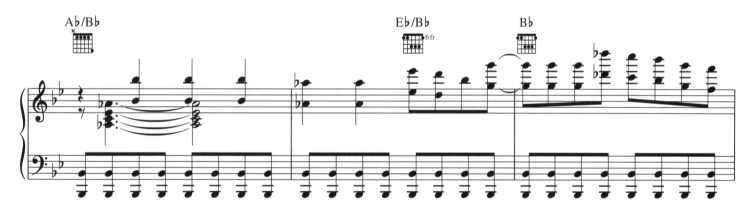

ZOSER:

He's ___ lost all sense ___ of rea - son

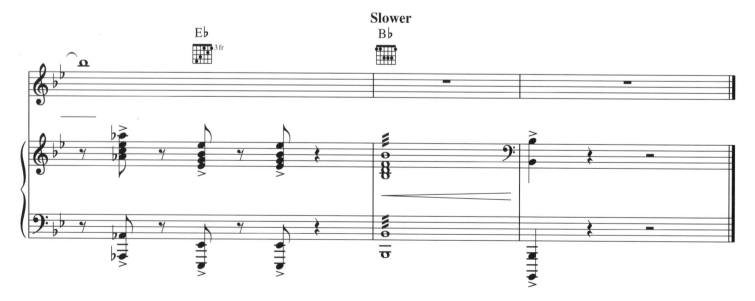

RADAMES' LETTER

Music by ELTON JOHN
Lyrics by TIM RICE

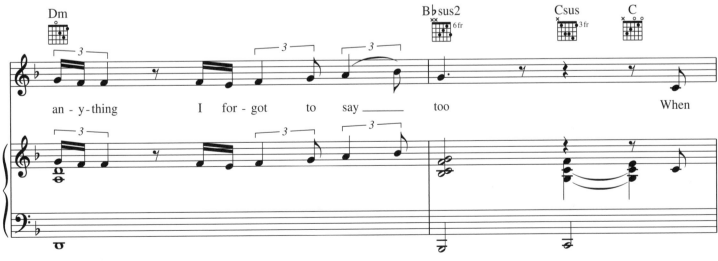

things get _ so com-pli-cat - ed I

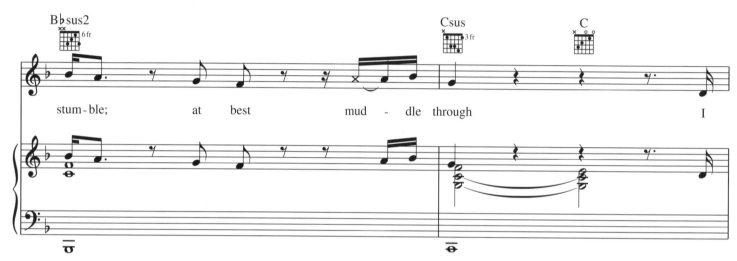

stum-ble; at best mud-dle through I

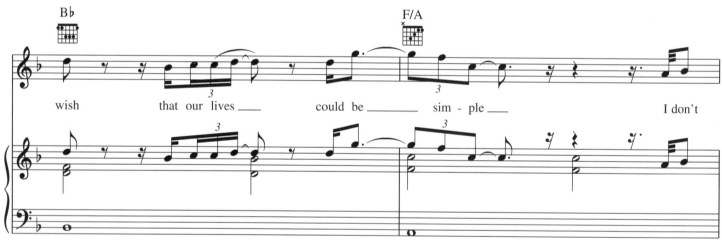

wish that our lives ___ could be _____ sim-ple ___ I don't

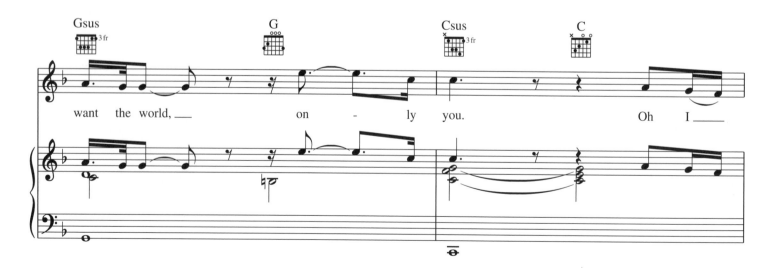

want the world, ___ on - ly you. Oh I ____

wish __ I could tell ___ you this face _____ to face _____ But _ there's

nev-er the time, nev-er the place _____ So this ___

let-ter will have _____ to do _____ I _____

love _____ you.

WRITTEN IN THE STARS

Music by ELTON JOHN
Lyrics by TIM RICE

RADAMES:

all ___ that we are good _ for just a stretch _ of mor-tal time? __

AIDA:

Or some

God's ex-per-i-ment __ In which we have no say?_____ In

which we're giv-en par-a-dise But on - ly for a day_____

I KNOW THE TRUTH

Music by ELTON JOHN
Lyrics by TIM RICE

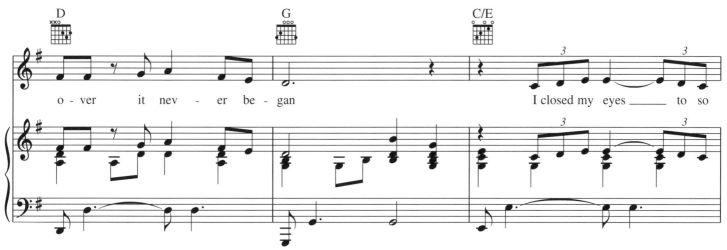

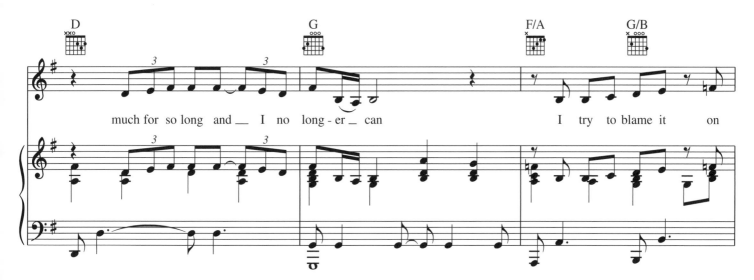

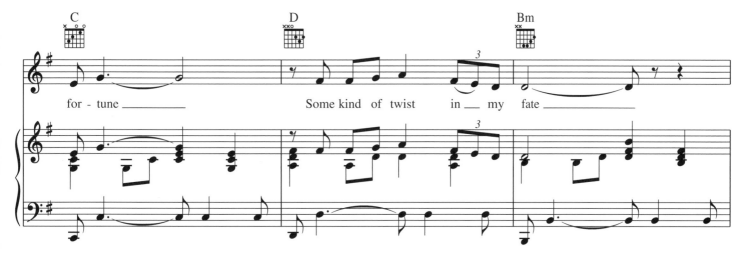

late

I know the truth ___ and it mocks me ___

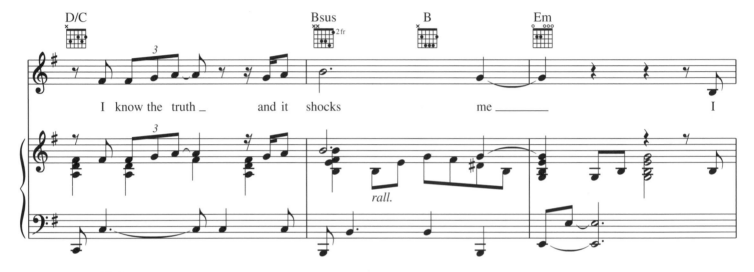

I know the truth ___ and it shocks me ___

rall.

I

Rubato

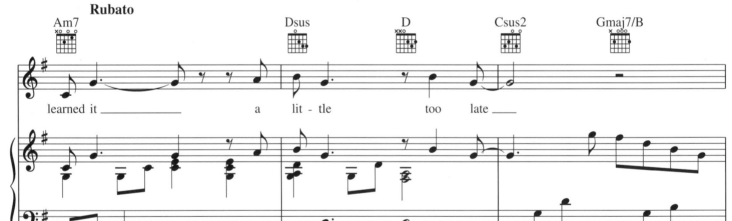

learned it ___ a lit - tle too late ___

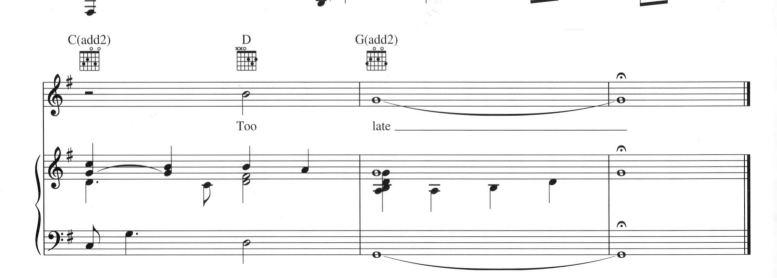

Too late ___